ELECTRICITY
AND
MAGNETISM

GREGORY VOGT

ELECTRICITY ─AND─ MAGNETISM

FRANKLIN WATTS
NEW YORK ■ LONDON ■ TORONTO ■ SYDNEY ■ 1985
A FIRST BOOK

Frontis: Generators at the Hoover Dam Powerplant.
The generator is a perfect symbol of the close
relationship between electricity and magnetism.

Diagrams by Vantage Art.

Photographs courtesy of:
Bureau of Reclamation: frontis;
New York Public Library Picture Collection: pp. 4, 60;
The Bettmann Archive: pp. 15, 47 (top and bottom);
Bakken Library of Electricity in Life: pp. 26, 36, 40–41;
Research Corporation: pp. 44, 45;
Con Edison: pp. 67, 68; Sony Corporation: p. 71.

Library of Congress Cataloging in Publication Data

Vogt, Gregory.
Electricity and magnetism.

(A First book)
Bibliography: p.
Includes index.
Summary: Discusses the discovery, fundamentals, and
uses of electricity and the closely related force,
magnetism. Also includes suggested experiments.
1. Electricity—Juvenile literature. 2. Magnetism—
Juvenile literature. [1. Electricity. 2 Magnetism]
I. Title
QC527.2.V64 1985   537   85-10565
ISBN 0-531-10038-3

CONTENTS

ELECTRICITY
AND
MAGNETISM

INTRODUCTION
ENERGY AT
YOUR FINGERTIPS

Two centuries ago, the American scientist and statesman Benjamin Franklin spoke of electricity and said, "Electrical fluid . . . may . . . be of use to mankind." It was one of the great understatements of all time. Ben Franklin had no idea how much the future world would come to depend upon electricity and its closely related force, magnetism. How could he know? How could anyone have dreamed that 200 years later the whole world would become invaded by an energy source so powerful that it would change the face of the earth, yet so convenient to use that it could be controlled by the push of a button? Today, few aspects of modern life are untouched in some way by electricity.

Every day we use electricity directly or indirectly in thousands of ways. In the morning, we awake to the music or alarm from an electric clock radio. We turn on electric lights, dry our hair with an electric blow-dryer, eat food cooked on an electric stove, wear clothes made of fabrics woven with electric machines and sewn together with others. We travel to school over roads built with machines powered by engines that ignite fuel with electricity and ride in a bus or car powered by a similar engine. We talk on the telephone, and our voices are carried by electric currents. We move data through computers with electricity, watch electric-powered television, and much more. Even this book was written on an electric word processor and printed using an electric printing press. The words from this page are transmitted from your eyes to your brain via electric impulses.

Although electricity is an important part of life, most people know little about it. The only time most of us care about electricity is when power lines blow down in a storm and the lights go out, or when the monthly electric bill arrives. Learning about electricity is important because of the major part it plays in our world. Learning about electricity is also fun and exciting. In fact, electricity is such an interesting subject that many people choose to go into careers having to do with electricity.

This book starts with some very basic ideas and discoveries and goes on to explain how electricity makes things run. You'll find answers to such questions as: What is electricity? Why do electric motors turn? How are electricity and magnetism related? What kind of jobs can electricity do? Why do we sometimes get shocks after walking across a carpet on a dry day? What causes lightning?

You'll also explore electricity yourself by performing the experiments suggested in this book. They are fascinating, fun, and easy to do. All you need is simple, inexpensive materials such as wire, metal, batteries, small light bulbs, and a pocket compass. You also need the ability to follow directions and the willingness to make up your own experiments when you come up with new ideas and questions. Not only will these experiments help you understand electricity better, but some may make good projects for science fairs.

CHAPTER ONE
MYSTERIOUS FORCES

Electricity and magnetism were discovered a long time ago. The discoveries were made thousands of years and many miles apart. For a long time no one suspected that the two discoveries were related, but as scientists conducted their experiments, they began to wonder. Was there indeed a relationship between electricity and magnetism? Scientists would not learn the answer to that question until the early 1800s!

ROCKS THAT ATTRACT IRON

The first discovery was probably made in China about 5,000 years ago. Someone discovered that certain rocks, containing the iron ore mineral we call *magnetite*, held a mysterious force that enabled the rock to attract and hold pieces of iron. A rock held over tiny bits of iron would make the bits leap into the air and stick to the rock. Furthermore, a thin needle-shaped piece of iron rubbed with this strange rock would gain that force, too, and attract other iron to itself.

Even more meaningful was the discovery that that same iron needle would now always point to the north when suspended from a string. The Chinese put this discovery to practical use. Chinese military commanders led their troops across the vast Chinese frontier with the aid of the north-pointing iron needle. The Chinese emperor

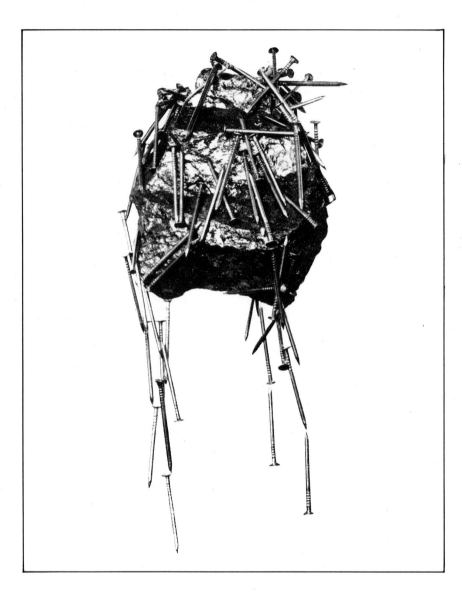

Lodestone, found in Arkansas

Huang-ti had a chariot built in 2637 B.C. that had the figure of a woman mounted on it. No matter which way the chariot traveled, the woman's outstretched arm always pointed north, presumably due to concealed bits of that mysterious rock. Strangely, more than 900 years passed before the Chinese thought to use the north-pointing needle to find their way across oceans.

The name for this mysterious force is *magnetism*, but the word isn't of Chinese origin. According to one story, a sheep herder named Magnes, who lived about 3,000 years ago in the Middle Eastern country of Magnesia, noticed that the iron nails in his shoes were attracted to a peculiar kind of rock. From either Magnesia or the shepherd's name, we get the word "magnetism."

The ability of magnetite to magnetize iron needles had an immense effect on the world. Using magnetic needles as compasses, sea captains could ply the oceans far from the sight of land and be sure of finding their way safely back to home port. By doing this, the world was opened to trade. Not only were goods traded, but so was knowledge; this helped people the world over improve the quality of their lives. Because magnetite enabled people to find their way, a special name was given to it: *lodestone*, which means "leading stone."

Sea captains kept a lodestone on board their ships and rubbed iron needles against it to make compasses. Lodestone was so valuable that sailors were punished for tampering with the ship's lodestone. One old sea law stated that a sailor could be punished by "having the hand which he most uses fastened, by a dagger or knife thrust through it, to the mast or principle timber of the ship. . . ." The punishment was harsh because tampering with the ship's lodestone could prevent the ship from returning home.

Through the years, many attempts have been made to explain the force of the lodestone. One strange theory was that the rock had many tiny invisible hooks that reached out and latched themselves onto any piece of iron. They held fast until they were pulled apart hard enough to break the hooks.

THE MYSTERIOUS POWER
OF AMBER

The second discovery was made 2,500 years ago by Thales of Miletus. Thales was a Greek astronomer and philosopher who, we are told, discovered a mysterious property of *amber*, tree sap that over thousands or millions of years had turned to stone, or been *fossilized*. Thales was rubbing a piece of amber with fur when he made his discovery. When rubbed with fur, the amber gained a mysterious power that enabled it to attract objects. Thales passed the rubbed amber over lint, bits of paper, and tiny pieces of feathers. The particles jumped into the air and stuck to the amber. After a while, those same particles fell away.

Thales attributed the mysterious power of amber to an inner soul. Amber was alive, he thought, and drew dead and nonliving material to itself as though it were actually breathing and sucking in air.

What had actually taken place was the result of static electricity. Incidentally, the word *electricity* comes from the Greek word for amber, which is *elektron.*

The discoveries of magnetism and static electricity must have been especially intriguing events in a world that had no television, radio, or movies. But, because of those discoveries, and hundreds of other discoveries by scientists over thousands of years, television and radio and so many other modern devices became possible.

EXPERIMENT 1
LODESTONE AND AMBER

If you would like to re-create the discoveries of the Chinese and of Thales, all you need to do is obtain some magnetite and amber. Both are prized by rock collectors, and you should be able to obtain them at rock shops or from someone who has a rock collection.

Rub the amber with fur and then see what it will attract. Try other materials besides fur to see if they will give amber a charge. Try magnetizing small metallic objects by rubbing them with the lodestone. Experiment with nails, screws, paper clips, coins, and pliers. (Incidentally, some of these may already be magnetized.) Also try magnetizing objects that have no metal in them. Are there objects you can't magnetize?

CHAPTER TWO

ATOMS, ELECTRICITY, AND MAGNETISM

To understand what magnetism and static electricity are, we must probe the secrets of the *atom*, the basic building block of our world. But what is an atom?

Imagine taking a lump of gold and dividing it in half. Then divide one of the halves in half. Do that again and again until you reach the smallest piece of gold possible. That piece is called an atom, and they are so small that 100 million of them lined up side by side would stretch out to no more than 1 inch (about 2.5 cm). Billions of them can fit on the head of a pin.

Atoms make up the more than 100 *elements* found on earth. An element is a substance containing only one kind of atom. An atom, therefore, is the smallest piece of any element that can still be recognized as that element. Gold is an element, and contains only atoms of gold. Oxygen, another element, is made up of only oxygen atoms. Silver, still another element, is composed of silver atoms only. And so on. Each type of atom has different characteristics, which is why the elements are all different—gold is heavy, has its unique color, is soft, etc.; oxygen is a colorless, odorless gas; and so forth. Elements can combine in many ways to make up all the solids, liquids, and gases that we call matter. For example, sodium can combine with chlorine to make salt.

If we carry our division of gold a step further and cut into the remaining single atom, we no longer have an atom of gold but the "pieces" that make up the atom, the stuff of the atoms themselves. There are three main pieces, called *subatomic particles*: protons, neutrons, and electrons. *Protons* and *neutrons* are found clustered in the center of the atom, which is called the *nucleus*. Moving around, or *orbiting*, the nucleus are one or more *electrons* (see Fig. 1). In this way, atoms resemble a miniature solar system. The nucleus is like the sun and the electrons are the planets. However, electrons do not move around the nucleus in neat paths the way the planets move around the sun. Rather, they swarm like a mass of bees in paths that are continually changing.

Before, we saw that each element has different characteristics and is therefore unique. An element is what it is because it has a special combination of protons, neutrons, and electrons. Hydrogen has only one proton and one electron. Helium has two protons, two neutrons, and two electrons. Oxygen has eight protons, eight neutrons, and eight electrons. Normally, the number of protons and electrons in each element is equal.

It is difficult to imagine how tiny an atom and its parts are. Think for a moment of an atom the size of a football stadium. The nucleus would be no larger than a pencil eraser and would be resting on the middle of the 50-yard line. The innermost electrons would be orbiting at about the 25-yard line, but most electrons would be orbiting among the outermost seats. You can see, then, that atoms are mostly just empty space!

Protons have a *positive charge*, as it is called. Electrons have a *negative charge*. Neutrons have no charge; they are "neutral."

ATOMS, CHARGES, AND ELECTRICITY

In order to understand electricity, we need to learn more about charges. What is a charge? It is difficult to answer this question, but you can get an approximate idea of what charges are by doing the following experiment.

Place two magnets near each other so that the north pole of one is pointing toward the south pole of the other. Cover the magnets

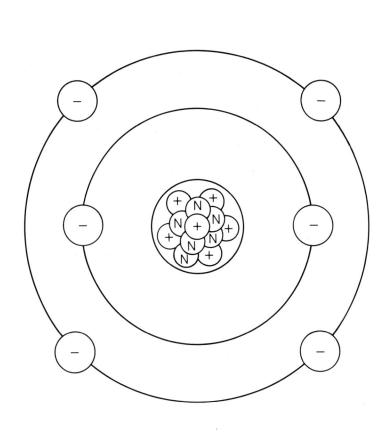

Fig. 1. The carbon atom has
six protons and six neutrons in its
nucleus and six electrons in orbit.

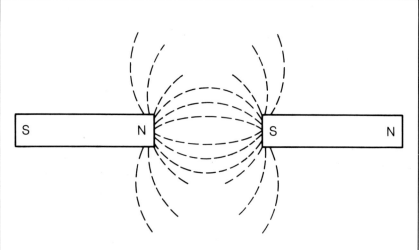

Fig. 2. When unlike poles of magnets are near each other,
the force lines of their magnetic fields join.

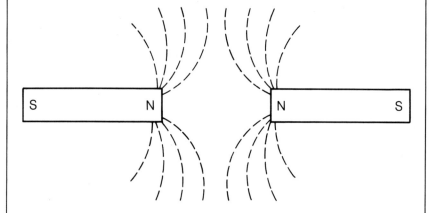

Fig. 3. When like poles of magnets are near each other,
the magnetic force lines push one another away.

with a sheet of white paper and sprinkle iron filings over the paper. (You can make your filings by rubbing iron nails with a metal file or by crumbling some steel wool into small fragments. Be careful not to get the bits of steel wool into your skin.) Tap the paper. The filings on the paper will arrange themselves in distinct lines. These are called *magnetic force lines* (see Fig. 2). The lines stretch neatly between the two magnets. Make a sketch of the lines.

Now remove the filings and change the magnets so that the two north poles or the two south poles are facing each other. Again sprinkle on the filings. This time, the lines do not join together (see Fig. 3) but actually push one another away. Make a sketch of these lines to compare with the first.

The force-line patterns in the experiment represent what happens with protons and electrons. The charge of the proton produces lines the same as the lines from the electrons. When a proton comes near an electron, the lines join together. When a proton comes near another proton or an electron near another electron, the lines push apart. In other words, (positive) protons attract (negative) electrons, but protons repel protons and electrons repel electrons. Unlike charges attract, and like charges repel.

Atoms are filled with charges, but because the number of protons and electrons are equal, the charges balance out and the whole atom has no charge, or is neutral. However, if an atom should give up or take on an extra electron, the atom itself is no longer neutral and is considered charged, or *ionized*. This can happen for a variety of reasons, such as when heat is applied to atoms or a magnet is moved near them. If an atom loses one electron, it then has more positive charges than negative charges and therefore the whole atom is considered positively charged. However, if an atom should take on an additional electron, the atom has more negative charges and is considered negatively charged.

When Thales was rubbing amber with fur, he was picking up electrons from atoms of the fur and transferring them to the surface of the amber. The amber had more electrons than it normally had so that it gained a negative charge which attracted the paper, lint, and feathers. The amber gained a charge of static electricity. Static electricity is simply *electric charges at rest*. An object that gains more electrons than it normally has or that has fewer electrons than normal is said to be charged with *static electricity*.

The attraction of an object with a negative static charge for a neutral object takes place because the extra electrons in the charged object repel some of the electrons in the neutral object. Those electrons move as far away as possible and the neutral object now has two charges, positive and negative. The negative charge of the first object now attracts the positive side of the second object, and the remaining negative charge on the second object repels the first object but less strongly. The attraction for a positive static charge is just the opposite of the first.

Incidentally, objects do not have to be solid to gain a static electricity charge. Clouds can build up tremendous static charges from violent movements of water drops and ice crystals because of wind. Eventually, the cloud tops and bottoms gain opposite static charges that lash out as lightning. When this happens, the charges balance themselves out again.

EXPERIMENT 2
CHARGING OBJECTS WITH
STATIC ELECTRICITY

Static electricity is easy and fun to work with. With some simple materials, you can learn about some of its properties.

MATERIALS:

hard-rubber comb
balloons
wool, fur, silk scarf, or flannel
puffed rice

Huge static buildups in clouds can lead to spectacular lightning displays.

Take the wool or other fabric you have chosen and vigorously rub the comb until you hear some small crackles. By rubbing, you are depositing electrons on the comb, which thereby gains a negative charge. Now bring the comb near some puffed rice or some bits of paper or lint. Why does the comb attract the puffed rice? What other materials will the charged comb attract? Try charging the comb by rapidly running it through your hair.

Blow up a balloon and tie it off. Now rub the balloon with the wool until the balloon is charged. Will the balloon attract the rice? Try sticking the balloon against a wall, the TV set, your head, etc. Will other materials, such as the fur of a dog or cat, give it a charge?

Blow up a second balloon and charge it also. Hold one balloon by the nozzle and bring the other charged balloon near it. Do they stick? Remember, like charges repel. Both balloons have a negative charge.

To show that the balloons are really charged with electricity, move one of the balloons near a fluorescent lamp tube while standing in a dark room. You should see a flicker of light inside the tube.

Static electricity experiments work best when the air is very dry. Moisture in the air helps electrons to leak away. You can find this out for yourself by running the shower in the bathroom with the door closed. Try charging a balloon there and see how long the charge lasts.

EXPERIMENT 3
MAKING A
STATIC ELECTRICITY DETECTOR

Static charges are easy to detect if you have the right equipment. You can make a simple static detector, called an *electroscope*, out of inexpensive materials.

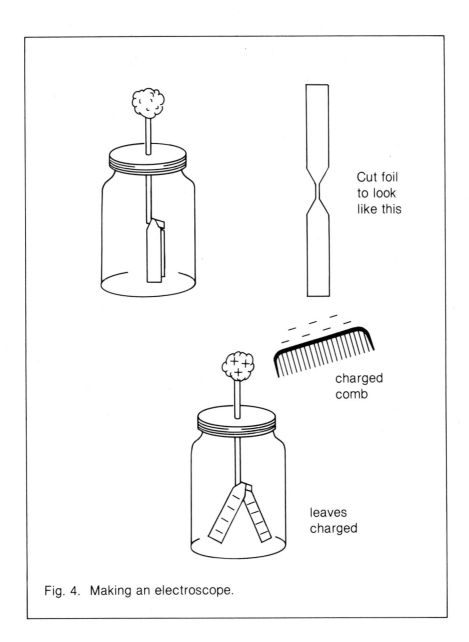

Cut foil
to look
like this

charged
comb

leaves
charged

Fig. 4. Making an electroscope.

clear glass jar with lid (a pickle jar will do)
rubber or cork stopper about 1 inch (2.5 cm) in diameter
heavy wire approximately 6 inches (15 cm) long
lightweight aluminum foil

Cut out a circular hole from the middle of the jar lid just smaller in diameter than the stopper. Drill a hole through the stopper just large enough to pass the wire through. Bend the wire at one end to form a small hook. If the wire has any paint or varnish on it, *scrape it off clean* with a knife or sandpaper. Insert the wire into the stopper and use the stopper to plug the hole in the lid. The hook should be about 2 or 3 inches (5 to 7.5 cm) off the bottom of the jar when the lid is screwed on.

Cut a thin strip of aluminum foil as shown in Fig. 4. Fold the strip and hang it on the hook inside the jar. Crumble some additional foil into a 1-inch (2.5-cm) ball and stick it over the other end of the wire. The electroscope is now ready to be used.

Bring a charged comb or other charged object near the aluminum ball but don't touch it yet. Watch what happens to the leaves inside the jar. The negative charge in the comb repels electrons in the ball. The electrons try to get as far away as possible and move into the foil leaves in the bottle. Because like charges repel, the leaves spread apart. When you move the comb away, the electrons return to the ball and the leaves hang straight down again.

Bring the comb near the ball again and this time touch the ball with it. The leaves fly apart again because of the negative charges. This time, however, some of the electrons from the comb move into the electroscope and remain when you take the comb away. The electroscope now has a negative charge because electrons moved into it when it was touched by the charged comb. They moved there to get away from one another.

Touch the ball with your finger to discharge the leaves. Electrons will travel from the leaves into your finger, so that the leaves are neutral again and they fall back together. Bring the charged comb near the ball again but do not touch them together. Touch the ball with a finger on your other hand after the leaves have spread apart. The leaves will come back together again because your finger has given the electrons a place to go that is even farther away than the leaves. Take your finger and the comb away. What happens? The aluminum ball is now missing some of its electrons, and electrons move up from the leaves to fill in some of the gaps. This causes the leaves to be positively charged, and they repel each other.

Take your uncharged electroscope and see what objects around your house have charges. Try the TV set screen when it is on and after it is turned off. Try clothes straight out from the dryer, plastic wrappers just after they are torn off from the boxes they surround, etc. **Do not probe near electrical outlets or into electrical appliances!** Remember, the electroscope has a wire that will conduct electricity and you could get a shock.

ATOMS AND MAGNETISM

We began this chapter by looking into the nature of the atom. You now know that static electricity is produced by objects gaining or losing electrons. But did you know that electrons are also the source of magnetism?

Although our world is made up of more than 100 elements, most of the things you come into contact with every day are not individual elements but *molecules.* A molecule is produced when two or more atoms link themselves together.

As the electrons orbit the nuclei of the atoms, the electrons spin on their axes. A good comparison to this is the motion of the members of our solar system. While the planets are orbiting our sun, they are also spinning. In the case of electrons, their spin creates a magnetic field around the electron. If you could pour iron filings around an electron that has its axis of spin pointing directly at you, the filings would line up along the magnetic force lines in neat circles. The magnetic force lines travel in clockwise or counterclockwise directions.

If two spinning electrons in a molecule come close to each other, their magnetic force lines either combine or cancel out. In most materials, the spins of electrons are in opposite directions and their magnetic fields cancel. Therefore, the material has no magnetic properties. However, in some materials the electrons spin in similar directions so that their magnetic fields are added on. The molecules in these materials are called *magnetic molecules.* Rocks that contain a large quantity of these magnetic molecules are magnetic. Magnetite, or lodestone, is such a rock.

Magnetism is really a much more complicated concept, but you now have a better idea why some materials possess magnetic properties. The important thing to remember is that electrons are responsible for both magnetism and electricity.

EXPERIMENT 4
EXPLORING MAGNETISM

Before we go on, it would be worthwhile for you to experiment with magnets. Take a magnet and see what materials it will attract. Try different kinds of metal, coins, wood, plastic, glass, and anything else you can think of (except magnetic recording tape, which can be ruined). What did all the objects attracted to the magnet have in common? Also experiment to see if magnetism will pass through objects. Lay a paper clip on a piece of cardboard and hold the magnet to the other side. Try to move the paper clip by just moving the magnet. If you have a strong enough magnet, you may even be able to move steel forks, knives, and spoons by sliding the magnet below the dinner table. Will a magnet work through your hand?

You also can learn about magnets by breaking them. If you have a magnet that you don't mind destroying, break it in half. Do both pieces still have magnetic properties? Does each piece have a north and south pole? How would you find out? Next, break one of the halves in half. How small can you make the pieces without losing the magnetism? You might figure out the answer to this question if you think about magnetic molecules. (If you don't want to break a good magnet, make a magnet out of an iron nail by rubbing it with a magnet about forty times in one direction. You can then break the nail magnet with a wire cutter.)

EXPERIMENT 5
MAKING A COMPASS

You have learned that iron needles can be magnetized by rubbing them against a piece of lodestone. Actually any magnet will do to magnetize a needle. By following these instructions, you can make a magnetic compass that actually works!

MATERIALS:

magnet
large sewing needle
cork stopper
dish detergent

Rub one end of the magnet on the sewing needle forty or fifty times. Rub the needle in the same direction each time. You are trying to coordinate the spin of electrons in the molecules inside the needle. You do not want to mix them up by rubbing two ways. Test your needle by bringing it near an unmagnetized piece of iron such as a carpet tack or a pin. If the needle attracts the iron, you are ready to go on.

Cut a piece of cork about ¼ of an inch (about 0.5 cm) thick. You may substitute some other floating material if you do not have a cork. The piece must be large enough to support the needle in the water.

Carefully slide the needle through the cork as shown in Fig. 5. You may also glue the needle if you wish.

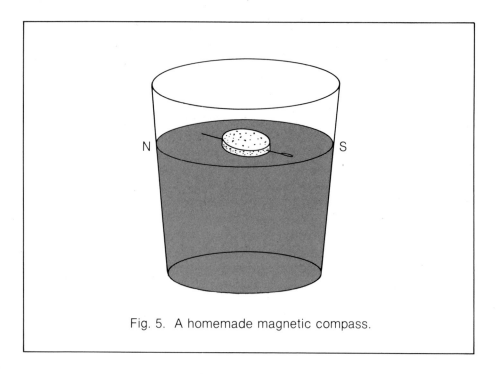

Fig. 5. A homemade magnetic compass.

Place a drop of dish detergent in the water. This helps the needle remain in the center. Carefully place the needle on the water surface. Observe the movement of the needle.

Why does the needle move? Because the needle is a magnet, it will align itself with the magnetic field of the earth. One end will always point north and the other south except when you bring something that is magnetic near it. The magnet you used to magnetize the needle will cause the needle to spin. Will an unmagnetized butter knife affect the needle? What other things will affect the needle? If you place the compass inside a box, will it still point north? Carefully take your compass outside into an open field. Take a sighting along the needle at some distant object. Then try to walk toward that object while looking only at the compass needle.

CHAPTER THREE

ELECTRICITY: A FLOWING STREAM

Under the right conditions, electrons can be made to flow from one place to another. When this happens, we have a second kind of electricity besides static—a *current.* That's what lightning is, and the electricity you get from your wall outlets at home. These moving electrons can be compared to a flowing stream of water. Similar words are even used to describe them, such as "flow" and "current." But, unlike water, electricity flows only when a complete *circuit,* or circle, exists, going from the source of the electricity through the device it powers, such as a light bulb, and back to the source (Fig. 6).

This flowing electricity, as we will see later, has many practical applications. It is the kind of electricity we use most often.

TRANSMITTING ELECTRICITY

Scientists first learned that electricity could be made to flow, or be *transmitted,* in the 1720s. The English scientist Stephen Gray, like other scientists of the time, was fascinated by static electricity and anxious to learn all he could about it. He knew that several materials, such as amber, sulfur, feathers, hair, silk, and linen, could be charged with static electricity by warming and rubbing them. He asked himself if metal could also be charged, a question that led him to perform a series of experiments that eventually proved electricity could be transmitted.

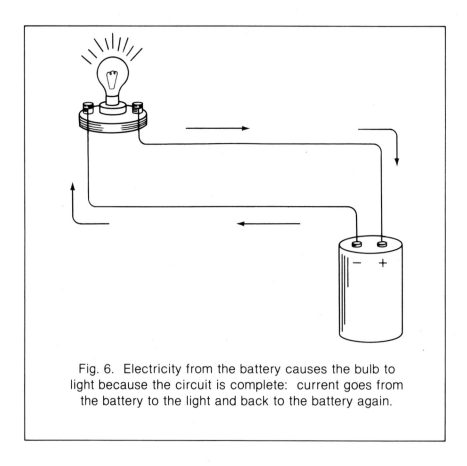

Fig. 6. Electricity from the battery causes the bulb to light because the circuit is complete: current goes from the battery to the light and back to the battery again.

Gray was not a rich scientist, and he could not afford the fancy apparatus and supplies other scientists of the time worked with. Working with simple materials, he began his studies by rubbing metal the way he did other materials. This first experiment was unsuccessful: the metal would not gain a charge. It then occurred to him that he might be able to electrify metallic objects simply by touching them with something already charged. He reasoned that the charged object would transfer its charge to the metal.

Gray began his new experiments by working first with materials he was familiar with. He fitted the ends of a 3½-foot-long (1 m) glass tube with corks to keep out the dust. When Gray charged the tube by rubbing it, the corks became charged also and attracted feathers. He then tried sticking one end of a wooden stick into one cork and placed an ivory ball on the other end of the stick. The ball became electrified, too!

Gray carried his experiments further by using longer sticks and then metal rods to transfer the charge from the tube. Gray soon ran into a problem. As his sticks and metal rods got longer, he had a difficult time bending them to fit into his laboratory. Gray then hit upon a solution. He would try to transmit charges through wool thread. This proved to be a very successful solution to the problem, and Gray and his assistant soon succeeded in transmitting electricity 765 feet (233 m) in one experiment!

No one knows whether Gray ever tried using flexible metal wire to transmit electricity. The technology for making metal wire was relatively new to England at the time, and Gray may have been unable to afford wire.

About ten years later, Charles Du Fay discovered that wet threads carried, or conducted, electricity much better than dry threads. The work of both Gray and Du Fay led Benjamin Franklin into trying his famous kite experiment.

Franklin was trying to learn if lightning and electricity were the same thing. In order to do that, he decided he had to "catch" some lightning. Franklin constructed a simple but dangerous experiment. During a thunderstorm, he and his son flew a kite high into the clouds. A metal key was tied to the lower end of the kite string.

In the rain, the kite string became wet. The wet string became an excellent electrical conductor! If lightning were electricity, the string would conduct it to where Franklin could observe it. As a dark thundercloud passed overhead, a static charge from the cloud was conducted along the wet string to the key. A spark leaped out from the key to Franklin's knuckle. By this, Franklin and his son demonstrated that lightning and electricity were one and the same. He and his son

Benjamin Franklin, doing his famous kite experiment

were lucky. If lightning had struck the kite, the bolt would have traveled down the string and the two would probably have been electrocuted. **Do not try to reproduce Franklin's kite experiment.**

HOW ELECTRICITY IS CONDUCTED

The discovery that electricity can be transmitted has become a commonplace part of life. Our landscape is crisscrossed with power, telephone, and cable television transmission lines, all carrying electricity. To understand the way these metal wires carry electricity, we have to go back to the idea of the flowing stream.

Electricity can flow only when a pathway exists. Materials that make good pathways are called *conductors.* Metals are usually good conductors and among the best metallic conductors are copper and silver. Materials that resist the flow of electricity are called *insulators.* Rubber, glass, and plastic are typical insulators.

Although a stroke of lightning lasts for only a fraction of a second, it, too, needs a pathway to travel. Air is normally a poor conductor of electricity. In fact, air is actually an insulator. However, lightning has so much energy that the air becomes a conductor. In a moment, we will see how this is possible.

If we could look deep into a piece of copper wire, into the atoms themselves, we would see that copper atoms share their electrons with one other. This is called *bonding.* An electron leaves one copper atom for another copper atom and then goes back to the first atom or moves on to another atom. The hole left by the electron, as it moves to another atom, is immediately filled by an electron from somewhere else. You might say that these electrons go "visiting." This visiting is what holds, or bonds, all the atoms together.

Normally, the motion of these wandering copper electrons is random. That is, they move from atom to atom in many different directions. When that is happening, no electricity is flowing through the copper. It is just copper's natural state. However, when an electric current is present, all these electrons move in the same direction. That is what happened when Gray and Franklin transmitted electricity through threads. The static charges they experimented with pushed electrons through the thread in a current.

Poor conductors of electricity contain few *free* electrons around their atoms, so that it is hard to make a current run through them. This is the case with air. However, if the electric current is strong enough, even the electrons in the atoms that make up air will conduct electricity. This is what happens with lightning.

EXPERIMENT 6
CONDUCTING ELECTRICITY
THROUGH THE AIR

You can demonstrate how electricity is conducted through the air by experimenting with a 6-volt lantern battery. Connect the bare end of a wire to one of the battery's terminals. Touch the other bare end of the wire to the other terminal for just a moment. You will hear a faint crackling sound. Do this in a darkened room and you will also see a very small spark leap through the air. If you connect several batteries together, you can get a bigger spark. The spark leaps a greater distance because the combined batteries produce more voltage. **Do not carry this experiment any further because more voltage than this can be dangerous!**

EXPERIMENT 7
MAKING A CURRENT DETECTOR

Current detectors are simple to make and useful in determining whether a battery can produce electricity or whether a circuit will carry a current. Current detectors work because of the magnetic fields electric currents produce.

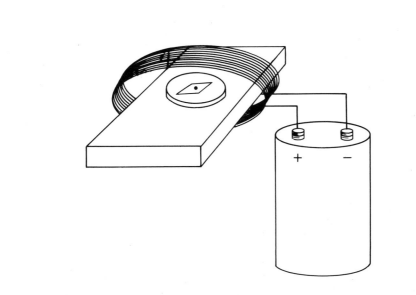

Fig. 7. A homemade current detector.

MATERIALS:

a magnetic compass
about 10 feet (3 m) of insulated wire
a 1.5-volt flashlight dry cell or 6-volt lantern battery

Using pliers, a knife, or wire stripper, cut about an inch (2.5 cm) of insulation off each end of the wire. Then start wrapping the wire around the compass in neat coils as shown in Fig. 7. Use all the wire for the coils except about 1 foot (30 cm) at either end. As you wrap the compass, try not to cover all of its face. You want to be able to see the needle. If you would like to make a more permanent detector, try mounting the compass on a block of wood before you wrap the wire into coils.

To use the current detector, touch the ends of the wires to the terminals of a battery. When a current runs through the wire, a magnetic field will be produced, which will cause the compass needle to move. Make sure you aim the detector so that the needle is parallel to the wire coils before you start.

Note which wire end you touched to the positive (+) terminal of the battery and which wire end you touched to the negative (−) terminal. Also note in which direction the compass needle moved. Now try reversing the wires and see which way the compass needle moves.

You will use the current detector in an experiment that follows in the next chapter. **Do not use the current detector on wall currents or any electrical appliances!**

CIRCUITS:
PATHWAYS OF ELECTRICITY

At the beginning of this chapter, you learned that electricity needs a complete circuit before a current will flow. Normally, a circuit consists of a wire going from a battery or a generator to the device it powers, such as a motor or a light bulb, and back to the battery or generator. If the circuit is broken, the current will stop (see Fig. 8). Often, it is desirable to break or open a circuit. For example, you break the circuit when you flip a switch to turn off the lights. The switch opens a gap in the wire so that electricity cannot flow.

Two kinds of electrical circuits are used most: series circuits and parallel circuits. In a *series* circuit, several electrical devices are wired end-to-end (see Fig. 9). Christmas tree lights used to be strung in series, so let's use an old-style Christmas light string as an example. Electricity travels through one light, then another, and another, and so on through the entire string of bulbs. The circuit works fine

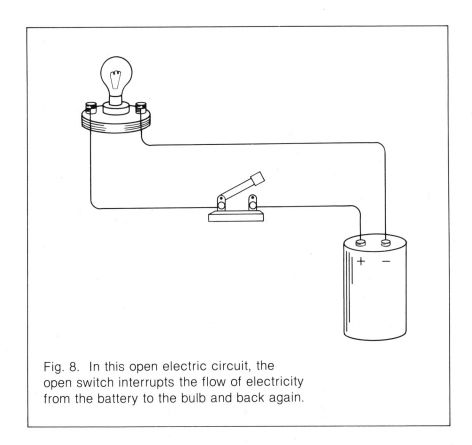

Fig. 8. In this open electric circuit, the open switch interrupts the flow of electricity from the battery to the bulb and back again.

until one bulb burns out. Then it is as though someone had flipped a switch. The burned-out bulb shuts off the entire string of bulbs. To solve this problem, manufacturers began to wire light strings in parallel circuits.

In a *parallel* circuit, each light is connected directly to the power source (see Fig. 10). All the lights go on together, but if one burns out, the other lights stay on. This is the kind of wiring you have in your house. With parallel circuits, you can turn on any number of

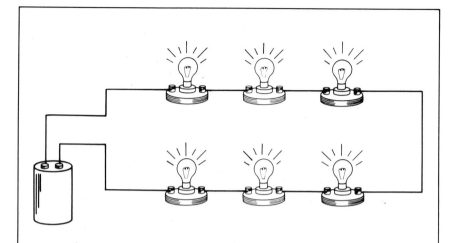

Fig. 9. In a series circuit, all the lights go on together.
If one bulb burns out, all the lights go out because the
burned-out bulb acts like an open switch.

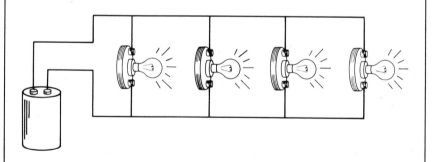

Fig. 10. In a parallel circuit, all the lights also go on together.
If one bulb burns out, however, the remaining bulbs stay lit.

appliances and lights and have them all run even if one light bulb burns out.

Although most wiring is done with parallel circuits, series circuits are still used. In a flashlight, for example, each battery is placed end-to-end. The electricity produced by one battery passes through the other battery or batteries in line. In this way, the batteries' power is multiplied and the bulb shines more brightly.

EXPERIMENT 8
SERIES AND PARALLEL CIRCUITS

The difference between series and parallel circuits is easily seen by trying the following experiments.

MATERIALS:

short pieces of electrical wire
three or four flashlight bulbs
one flashlight dry cell (battery)

Prepare each bulb so it can be wired into the circuit you are about to make. A wire must touch the two contacts of each bulb. This can be done in a number of ways. You can tape, glue, or solder the wires in place or make some sort of socket to hold them. It's up to you. You must also fix two wires to the contacts of the dry cell.

In the first experiment, splice the wires together so that your circuit looks like that shown in Fig. 9. This is a series circuit. Now, disconnect one of the bulbs. What happens?

In the second experiment, construct the circuit shown in Fig. 10. This is a parallel circuit. Now, disconnect one of the bulbs. What happens?

THE PATH OF LEAST RESISTANCE

As you know already, some materials are better conductors of electricity than others. If electricity is given a choice between two wires, it will always travel through the wire that offers the least *resistance* to its passage—the wire made of the best conductor. Look at resistance this way. Which is easier, walking through an open door or crashing through the wall? You can get through both ways, but one way is much harder than the other. Like you, electricity will choose the easiest pathway.

The path of least resistance is an important concept to remember. Electricity can kill you if you do the wrong thing, like trying to use a hair dryer while taking a bath or touching a light fixture while standing in water. If your body completes an electric circuit, electricity might find it easier to travel through you than through the electric appliance you are touching. The thing to remember is to never let your body complete an electric circuit, especially when you are standing in water.

CHAPTER FOUR
MAKING ELECTRICITY

As scientists learned more and more about electricity, they began to discover new ways to produce it. It became possible to generate electricity with chemicals, static electricity machines, and *generators*—machines that generate electricity with magnetism. Each of these methods was the result of interesting discoveries.

FROM FROG LEGS TO BATTERIES

Sometimes, rather unlikely events have great consequences for the future. One such event happened to the scientist Luigi Galvani. In 1780, Galvani was dissecting a frog in a laboratory also used for electrical experiments. While he was probing the frog's legs with a steel scalpel, an assistant produced a spark from a nearby static electricity machine. The frog's legs suddenly twitched. That discovery began Galvani on an investigation of what he wrongly called ''animal electricity.''

In one of his many experiments, Galvani hung some legs of freshly killed frogs on a brass hook over an iron fence during a thunderstorm. Whenever the legs drooped down and touched the iron fence, the muscles in the legs contracted, pulling them away from the iron. This happened even when lightning did not strike. Galvani believed that animals contained electricity, but what really happened was that the moisture in the legs enabled chemical reactions to take place

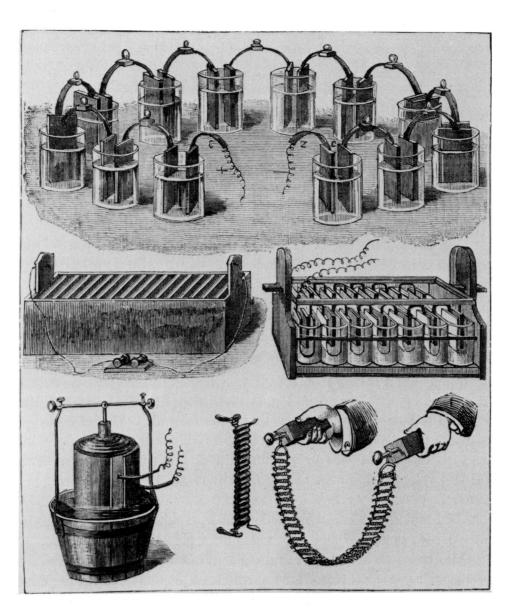

Old batteries

with the iron and brass, generating an electric current. The current triggered the twitching of the leg muscles.

Twenty years later, Alessandro Volta carried Galvani's discoveries an important step forward. Volta is credited with the invention of chemical batteries, which produced an easy-to-use, long-lasting source of electricity whenever a scientist needed it. In 1800, Volta stacked alternating disks of silver and zinc and sandwiched them between pieces of saltwater-soaked pasteboard. This arrangement caused a chemical reaction between the silver, zinc, and saltwater that produced a noticeable electric current. Thus was born an early version of the modern-day battery.

There are many kinds of modern batteries. One of the most common is the *wet cell*. The wet cell is used as the battery under the hood of an automobile. In a wet cell, chemical reactions create a flow of electrons that starts in a strong acid and moves through metal pieces called electrodes. This current then leaves the cell through one of the terminals so that it can be used (see Fig. 11). In your automobile, the electricity from the battery is carried to the starter motor (which is connected to the battery at the terminals). The starter motor begins to spin, and this turns the engine so that the car starts.

Another familiar battery is the *dry cell*, which is used in flashlights and portable radios. Actually, the term "battery" is improper here (although commonly used). When only one positive and one negative electrode are involved, the correct term is "cell." If two or more cells are joined together, the word *battery* is used. By the way, dry cells are not actually dry; they contain a wet paste. This eliminates the possibility of acid leakage when tipped upside down.

STATIC ELECTRICITY MACHINES

The battery invented by Volta in 1800 produced the world's first steady supply of electricity. Now scientists could begin to successfully investigate the properties of electricity. The only drawback to Volta's chemical battery, a drawback that still exists in the modern

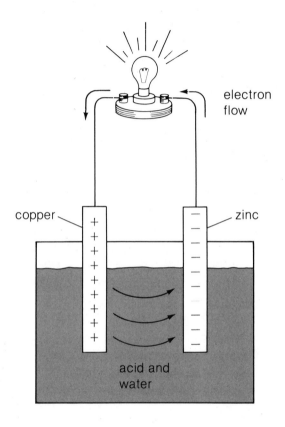

Fig. 11. In this wet cell, electrons flow to the zinc electrode,
which becomes negative. The copper electrode then becomes
positive. Electrons begin a current, leaving the zinc electrode
through the wire and returning to the copper electrode.

batteries of today, is that eventually the chemicals in the battery will be exhausted and the current flow will stop.

Volta's invention of the battery was possible because Galvani discovered a chemical reaction that produced electricity in frog legs. Galvani's discovery was possible because someone before him invented a static electricity machine, and static electricity machines were the result of a search by many scientists over centuries for an electricity-producing machine.

Static electricity machines produce a charge of static electricity by stripping off electrons from one material and transferring them to another. Eventually the collecting material has such a strong charge that a spark leaps with a loud snap from the collector to some nearby object.

One early static electric generator was invented by Wiliam Watson in the time of Volta. In Watson's experiments a girl rested her hand on a sulfur ball as it was rotated by a crank. Electrons picked up from the girl's hand transferred to the sulfur and then to the feet of a boy hung by silk ropes from the ceiling. The boy, in turn, touched the hand of a second girl standing on an insulated platform, and the electrons moved to this girl. With extra electrons, the girl built up a strong negative charge and was able to attract bits of seed chaff with her other hand.

Other static electricity machines invented later also worked by moving electrons from one material to another. The Wimshurst machine, invented in 1878 and still used today, mainly in science classrooms, uses two large glass plates that rotate in opposite directions. Static charges are picked up off these plates and transferred to glass and metal *Leyden jars.* Leyden jars, invented years before the Wimshurst machine, act as energy storage devices; one Leyden jar picks up a negative static charge while the other gains a positive charge. The electricity stored in the jars can be given off either as a big spark leaping through the air or as a steady trickle of electricity. Wimshurst machines were used in the 1890s to power early X-ray machines for doctors. They were later replaced by more reliable generators.

An old static electricity generator

In 1929, Robert Van de Graaff invented an especially powerful static electricity machine, which was called the Van de Graaff generator, after its inventor. The generator consists of a base in which electrons are deposited on a rubber belt. The electrons are carried up through a plastic or glass tube to the inside surface of a metal ball. Electrons, repelling one another, immediately move to the outside of the ball and come to rest. Depending upon the size of the metal ball, enormous amounts of electricity can build up. Van de Graaff generators have been adapted to all sorts of uses, including powering atom smashers that can split atoms into pieces for scientists to study.

GENERATORS THAT TURN
MAGNETISM INTO ELECTRICITY

When you look at a coin you see two sides. Each side is different, but only in appearance. It doesn't matter which side of the coin you see because you still recognize it as a coin. Electricity and magnetism are like the sides of that coin. They are only different sides of one force. Both are produced within the atom by the particles that make it up. Years ago, scientists only suspected there was a relationship between electricity and magnetism. No one knew how to prove it until Hans Christian Oersted conducted a classic experiment for a group of students in 1820.

Several years before, in 1813, Oersted reasoned that if electricity and magnetism were related, an experiment could be devised to demonstrate that relationship. He decided to find out whether an electric current would affect a magnetic compass. If it did, the compass needle would move. Oersted placed a compass on a table in his laboratory and stretched a wire over the compass needle. Then he sent an electric current through the wire. Much to his amazement, the needle did not move. Oersted sadly concluded that magnetism and electricity were two entirely different things.

For years, Oersted continued to believe in the results of his experiment. Then, in 1820, he decided to repeat his experiment for

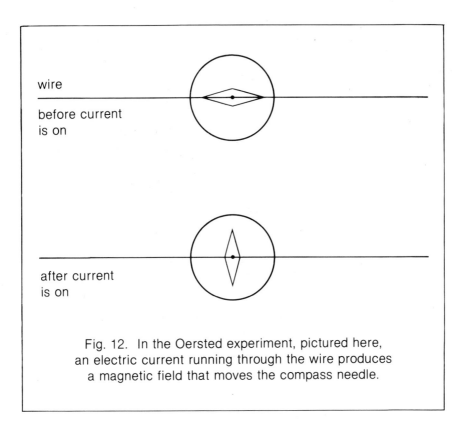

wire

before current
is on

after current
is on

Fig. 12. In the Oersted experiment, pictured here,
an electric current running through the wire produces
a magnetic field that moves the compass needle.

his students. During class, he set up the experiment again and ran a current through the wire. This time the compass needle moved! Oersted was astounded. A relationship existed after all.

The second experimental outcome resulted from a subtle but important change Oersted made in the way he set up his equipment the second time. In the first experiment, the compass needle was directly across or perpendicular to the wire before the wire was electrified. In the second experiment, it was parallel to the wire. Oersted learned that the magnetic field of an electrified wire causes a compass needle parallel to a wire to move to a perpendicular position. In

Van de Graaff generators at the Massachusetts Institute of Technology. Not all Van de Graaffs are this large; some will fit on a table top. Compare the electrical discharges with the lightning display shown earlier.

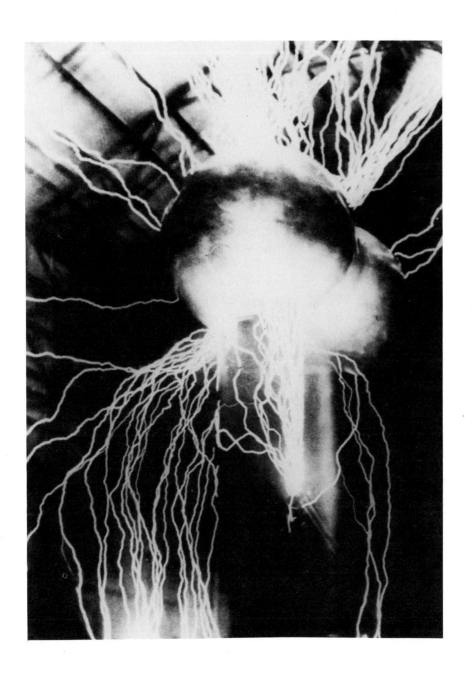

the first experiment, the needle was already perpendicular to the wire and therefore did not have to move to get there.

You can reproduce Oersted's famous experiment with the compass you used to make the current detector in the last chapter. Oersted used only one wire, so you should remove the compass from the wire coil for this experiment. Place the compass on a flat surface. When the needle stops moving, lay a copper wire directly over the compass face. Place the wire so that it is perpendicular to the compass needle. Connect the ends of the wire to a battery and watch what happens. Next, lay the wire over the compass face so that it is parallel to the needle. Again run current through the wire and watch what happens (see Fig. 12).

In 1830, Joseph Henry, working in America, discovered that magnetism could produce electricity! Henry produced a small, short-lasting electric current when he moved a wire within the field of a powerful magnet. A year later, Michael Faraday, working in London, made the same discovery.

The discovery made by these two scientists was simple but very important. The magnetic field reached into the moving wire to the atoms themselves and repelled electrons out of their orbits. As a result, the electrons moved in a continuous stream or current along the wire to make electricity. From this, it was a brief step to the invention of a device that would produce electricity using the principle discovered by Henry and Faraday: the alternating current generator.

Up to now, all electricity used by scientists in their experiments had been of the direct current variety. That meant the electrons flowed in one direction only, from the negatively charged end of the battery or electrostatic generator to the positive end.

Alternating current (AC) changes direction: the electrons travel in one direction through the wire and then alternate and travel in the other direction. The number of times the current changes from one direction to the other and back again in a second is its *frequency*. One such set of changes (one way and back) is one *cycle*. A frequency of 1 cycle per second is called a *hertz*. The electricity you

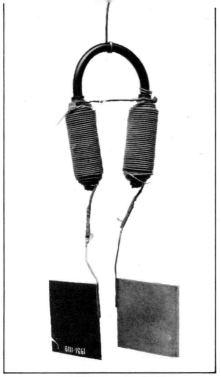

*An electromagnet
built by Joseph Henry*

*Michael Faraday,
lecturing at
the Royal Society
in England*

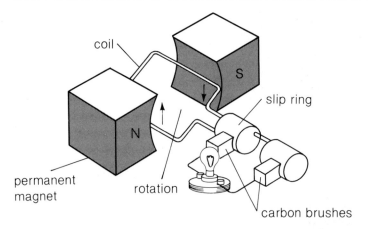

Fig. 13. In an alternating current generator, the magnets repel electrons in an electric current through the rotating wire. Each time the wire turns over, the current alternates, or changes direction.

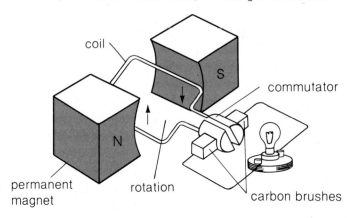

Fig. 14. The direct current generator works in a manner similar to that of the alternating current generator. However, the commutator prevents the electricity from changing direction each time the rotating wire flips over.

use from the wall outlets at home is 60-hertz AC. During each second, the current goes through 60 complete cycles.

The principle of the alternating current generator is very simple. A wire coil is mounted on a rotating shaft placed within the field of one or more magnets. As the wire coil is rotated, electrons are repelled by the field of the magnets and move from the coil to the outside of the generator. The magnetic field always pushes the electrons in the same direction. However, the moving coil keeps flipping over as it rotates. Therefore, the electrons in the flipping wire coil move in one direction and then the other (see Fig. 13).

A simple AC generator has one problem. The wires coming out from the rotating coil will wind onto the shaft and eventually break. To keep this from happening, electrical slip rings are attached to the wires of the coil. As the coil turns, wires from the outside rest or brush against the metal rings. In this manner, the electric current is passed to the outside of the generator without wrapping the wires around the shaft.

A slight change in the design of the alternating-current generator made it possible to build a direct current (DC) magnetic generator. The change was in the electrical contacts from the rotating wire coil inside the generator to the outside. The two slip rings on the rotating shaft were replaced by a split ring. One of the coil wire ends touched one half of the split ring while the other wire end touched the other half. Two brushes rubbed against the split ring as the shaft rotated. Each half-rotation caused the two split ring pieces to trade places and touch the other brushes. Because of this arrangement, the current did not alternate directions. Each time the current was about to alternate, the connections between the split rings and the brushes would be broken. The current would continue in the same direction (see Fig. 14).

Most electricity we use today is produced by mechanical generators of the AC variety. Electric power companies usually use large coal furnaces or nuclear power plants to produce steam that turns special fanlike blades called *turbines*. The rotating turbines turn the generators. Other power companies use the pressure of water held behind large dams to turn generators. Whatever the method used, huge quantities of electricity are produced with these generators, and that has made electricity available to nearly everybody.

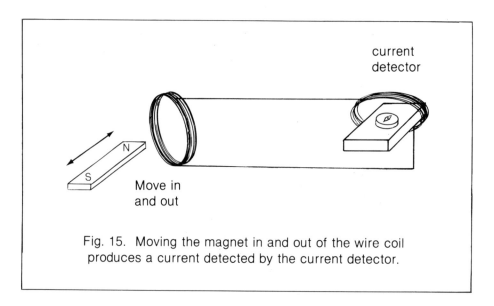

Fig. 15. Moving the magnet in and out of the wire coil produces a current detected by the current detector.

EXPERIMENT 9
THE HENRY/FARADAY EXPERIMENT

In this experiment, you will need the current detector you made in the last chapter. The detector will help you detect any currents you produce in the experiment.

MATERIALS:

current detector
bar magnet
coil of insulated wire

Use a knife or a wire-stripping tool to remove the insulation from the ends of the wire coil, and splice the ends to the wire leads of the current detector. Rapidly slide the bar magnet in and out of the wire coil (see Fig. 15). As you do this, watch the current detector compass needle. What happens?

You will notice that the current flows only when the magnet is moving. Do you think there will be any difference in the current if you hold the magnet still and move the coil? Can you think of any device that will keep the magnet or the coil moving so that the current will continue without stopping?

CHAPTER FIVE
MEASURING ELECTRICITY

Now that you know what electricity is and how it can be generated, let's learn a few words used in describing electricity. Look on the back or bottom of any appliance and you will see numbers and terms like 115 volts, 3 amps, and 150 watts. They tell you how much electricity the appliance will use. They are important terms, but many people often misunderstand what they mean. If you came in contact with 150,000 volts of electricity, would it harm you? The answer to that question depends upon a number of conditions. Just what do terms like volts and amps mean?

VOLTAGE

In a wire, electricity will flow only if two conditions are met. First, there has to be a complete circuit going from the source of the electricity, through the device it powers, and back to the source. Without that complete circuit, the electricity will flow for only a fraction of a second before it stops.

The second condition is that there has to be what scientists call a *potential difference* between the two ends of the wire.

Imagine a U-shaped tube with a valve at the bottom. One side of the tube is filled with water, and the other side is nearly empty (see Fig. 16). What will happen if the valve is opened? Water from the high side will rush through the valve to fill the lower side. When the two sides are equal, the water flow stops. Before the valve was opened,

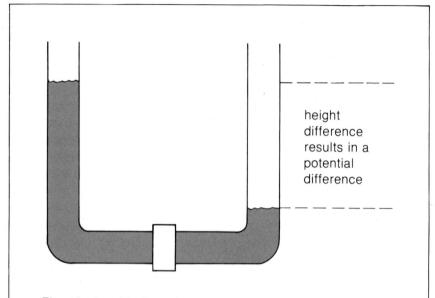

Fig. 16. In a U-shaped water tube, the difference in the two water heights results in a potential difference. When the valve at the bottom is opened, the water levels in the two tubes readjust.

there was a potential difference between the two water levels. This caused the water to flow when the valve was opened. When the water levels became equal, the potential difference was gone and the flow stopped.

With electricity, the potential difference is caused by a difference in the charges at the ends of the wire produced by a battery or generator. One end of the wire has more electrons than normal, and the other end has fewer electrons than normal. The difference in charges on the two ends acts like the difference in elevation of the water in the two ends of the tube. With electricity and with water, the greater the difference, the more pressure is in the line. *Voltage* is a measure of the electrical pressure in a wire that causes electrons to flow. A *volt* is the unit used to measure that pressure just as an inch or a centimeter is a measure of distance.

CURRENT

When people hear about high voltages, they generally become frightened. However, high voltage alone isn't enough to harm you if you receive a shock. In winter, when you drag your feet across the carpet you scrape up electrons from the carpet so that you become charged. You have established a large potential difference between you and your surroundings. If you touch a metal doorknob or some other metal object, electrons flow outward from you to balance the charges. The shock you receive when the spark leaps out from your finger is between 5,000 and 10,000 volts. However, the only sensation you get is an annoying snap in your fingertip. To be dangerous, there also must be a large *current*, or amount of electricity, flowing through the circuit in a given time.

Current is measured in *amperes*, or *amps* for short. Amperes measure the actual number of electrons going through a wire at any given time. In a 1-ampere circuit, about six and one-quarter billion billion electrons will pass a point each second! Fortunately, you don't have to count electrons yourself to measure *amperage*, or the number of amperes. Instruments called *ammeters* do that for you.

Earlier, we wondered if 150,000 volts of electricity was dangerous. It is if it is backed up with high amperage. If the amperage is low, 150,000 volts is not dangerous. You might think of it like getting hit in the face with a 100-mile-per-hour (161-km/hour) marshmallow—all speed but no punch. A 100-mile-per-hour rock is a different matter. High amperage is like the rock. Voltage and amperage together produce a dangerous combination.

RESISTANCE

Not all materials are good conductors of electricity. *Resistance* is the quality of a material that inhibits the flow of electricity, and it is a third important measurement in electricity. Resistance is measured in *ohms.*

To understand what resistance is, let's go back to the U-shaped water tube. When one side of the tube has more water than the other, there is a pressure inside the tube. If the valve at the bottom is opened, the water from the high side will flow into the low side. If the valve at the bottom is opened all the way up, there is little resistance to the flow of water. But if the valve is opened only partially, the water cannot flow as rapidly through the tube. The valve offers resistance to the flow. The same kind of thing takes place in electric wires.

To some extent, all materials offer some resistance to electricity. Materials which contain large numbers of free electrons in them, such as some metals, have the least resistance. Thick wire has less resistance than thin wire of the same material. Think of a wire as a pipe. A thick pipe has more room for the electrons to flow. Wire length is another factor. Electrons have to flow farther through long wires and therefore encounter more resistance. Still another factor is temperature. Certain metals offer less resistance at low temperatures, while other materials become better conductors at higher temperatures.

POWER

Power is the rate or speed at which work is done. If you could lift 550 pounds of bricks or anything else 1 foot (0.3 m) into the air in 1 second, you would be doing 1 horsepower of work. In electricity, the power—the rate at which appliances do work—is measured in *watts.*

You are used to seeing the power of light bulbs written in watts. For example, a 100-watt bulb uses 100 watts of electricity, which means the bulb works to produce a certain amount of light and heat each second. An electric motor rated at 746 watts does 1 horsepower of work in a second.

Electric power companies measure your energy use when they figure out your monthly bill. The unit they use is the *kilowatt-hour* (a kilowatt is 1,000 watts, since *kilo* means "thousand"). You might want to think of a kilowatt-hour as equivalent to the amount of electric power used by ten 100-watt bulbs for one hour. Kilowatts and hours, rather than watts and seconds (watts measure energy use per second), are used because otherwise huge numbers would have to be used—which would be very inconvenient. (For example, 1 kilowatt-hour equals 360,000,000 watt-seconds.)

Many people complain about the high cost of electric bills. It is important to remember that the more electricity you use, the more you have to pay. To reduce the monthly cost of electricity, you have to reduce the amount of electricity you use.

You can save money on electricity by doing a number of things. Turn off unnecessary lights, since leaving lights on in rooms no one is using is a big energy waster. Use lower-wattage bulbs in your lamps. Shut off TV sets and radios when they are not being used. Check the power ratings of your appliances and avoid using the ones that have the highest ratings in watts. Big power users are usually the ones that turn electricity into heat or use electricity for cooling: air conditioners, toasters, irons, and hair blow-dryers. When large appliances are being purchased, such as refrigerators and washing machines, check for the EER, or *energy efficiency rating*. That rating will tell you how much electricity the appliance is likely to use. Buy appliances that have lower ratings.

There is much more you can do to save electricity, and many electric power companies are glad to offer suggestions on how to save electricity. As an interesting experiment, find out what your family pays for electricity each month. Then, challenge everyone in the family to find ways of saving electricity so that the monthly bills will be lower. Set a goal of reducing electricity consumption by 10 percent. To be fair in this experiment, you should compare last year's bills with this year's bills because each month of the year produces different weather and daylight conditions. If you have an electric air conditioner in your house, you cannot accurately compare the electric use of the month of July with the month of October. Rather, compare July of one year with July of another.

CHAPTER SIX
USING
ELECTRICITY

Although electricity is used daily in thousands of ways, most of its uses fall into three categories: to power electric motors to produce motion, to produce heat and light, and to carry information.

PRODUCING MOTION

Electric motors work because electricity can produce magnetism. To understand how electricity produces motion in electric motors, it is first important to understand what electromagnets are, since they make up the "heart" of motors.

An electromagnet is basically a coil of wire wrapped around an iron core. When the electricity is turned on, the current produces a strong magnetic field that surrounds the electromagnet. This is what Oersted showed us in his famous experiment. Usually the field lasts as long as the current is moving through the wire. Like the permanent magnets you have been experimenting with, electromagnets have north and south poles. Unlike permanent magnets, however, the magnetic field disappears entirely when the current is turned off.

Electric motors essentially consist of two or more magnets that interact with each other to produce motion. At least one of those two magnets should be an electromagnet so that the poles of its magnetic field can be quickly reversed.

*Commercial electromagnet. Compare this picture
with that of the lodestone in Chapter 1.*

As you will see, electromagnets act like permanent magnets (magnets that hold their magnetism for a long time) in that they attract and repel. If we bring two electromagnets together so that their north poles are facing each other, these magnets will repel each other. If one of these magnets is fixed so that it cannot move and the other is mounted so that it can spin like a compass needle, the moving magnet will turn so that its south pole faces the other magnet.

Now, if we reconnect the wires from a battery to the fixed electromagnet, making the current direction change, that magnet's poles will reverse and north will become south and south will become north. This means that the south poles of the two magnets are now facing each other and they again repel each other. The spinning magnet moves again. If each time the spinning magnet makes one-half of a turn the other magnet reverses its poles, the spinning magnet will keep spinning. This is the principle of the electric motor.

EXPERIMENT 10
ELECTROMAGNETS

Electromagnets have two parts. The first is the coil of wire, called a *solenoid*. You can make a solenoid by loosely wrapping some copper wire around a pencil or larger cylindrical object. Slide the wire off the object and you have a solenoid. When a current is sent through the solenoid, a magnetic field is produced. You can detect this field by passing it near a magnetic compass.

The second part of an electromagnet is the iron rod placed within the solenoid. The rod intensifies the magnetic field. You can see this by sliding some iron nails between the flattened coils of the solenoid you just made. The iron nails intensify the field strength by bringing the force lines closer together.

You can make a good electromagnet by wrapping about fifty turns of insulated wire around a thick iron nail or bolt. Connect the wire to a dry cell and you have an electromagnet. Keep in mind that the electromagnet will drain your battery very rapidly, so do not leave it connected too long. Check the field of your electromagnet with paper and iron filings. See what the magnet will pick up. Will the magnet get stronger if you wrap more or fewer turns of wire around it?

EXPERIMENT 11
MOTORS AND MAGNETS

Try this simple experiment to understand how electric motors work. You will need an electromagnet and a bar magnet. Suspend the bar magnet with thread from some sort of wood frame like the one shown in Fig. 17. Connect the electromagnet to the battery as shown and bring one of the magnet's poles near the bar magnet. One pole of the bar magnet will immediately swing toward the electromagnet. Don't let them touch. Now, quickly reverse the electromagnet's wires on the battery terminals. This will reverse the current direction in the magnet and reverse its poles. What happens to the bar magnet? Keep switching the wires on the battery terminals so that each time the bar magnet swings to a new position, it is again repelled. See how fast you can get the bar magnet spinning.

DC MOTORS

DC motors have four main parts. The innermost part is the *armature*, an electromagnet that can spin on an axle. Surrounding the armature is a *field coil*, which is a second electromagnet, but one which doesn't move. When electricity enters the wires of the field coil and magnetizes it, one end becomes north and the other south. The armature also receives a current and therefore gets a north and south pole. The armature will immediately move so that its north pole is near the south pole of the field and its south pole near the north

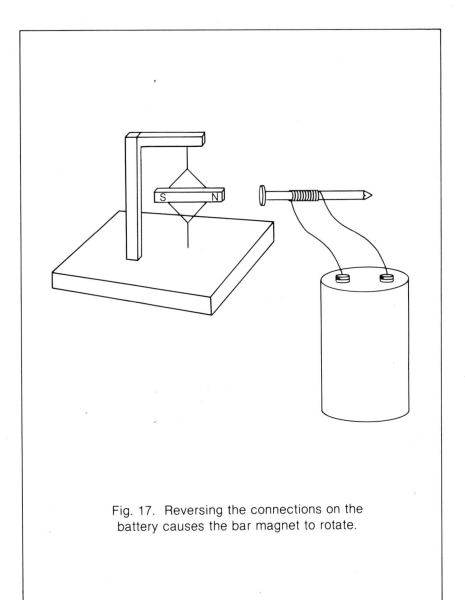

Fig. 17. Reversing the connections on the
battery causes the bar magnet to rotate.

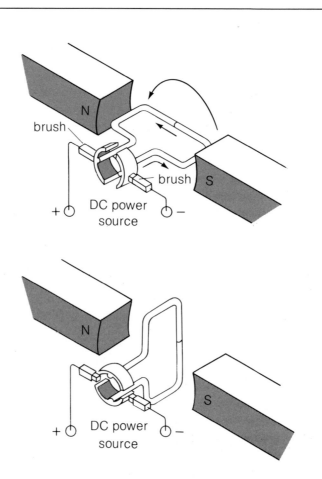

Fig. 18. A simple direct current motor is just a direct current
generator worked in reverse. An electric current is sent
through the wire, and the magnetic field produced rotates
the wire within the fields of the two permanent magnets.

pole of the field. At that point, the armature will stop unless the poles on the armature can be reversed as was done with the electromagnet in the previous experiment. If this happens, the armature will be repelled by the field and move to a new position. If the armature poles can be reversed again, the armature will keep on moving. And so on. This is precisely what happens in a DC motor.

To reverse the poles of the armature, two devices are used. One is a split metal ring around the armature shaft, called the *commutator*. The ends of the wires wrapped around the armature terminate in the two halves of this ring. Each wire touches only half of the ring. Electricity enters the armature through a second device called *brushes*, electrical contacts that rest against, or brush, the commutator pieces. As the armature rotates, the commutator pieces spin under the brushes. Each brush touches one commutator piece and then the other. In this manner, the electrical circuit of the armature is reversed every half-turn. The current travels in one direction through the armature and then the other. This reverses the poles of the armature electromagnet so that the armature keeps spinning within the field coil magnet (see Fig. 18).

Electric motors are a useful way of putting electricity to work. With the rotational power drawn from the armature shaft, you can do many things. A modern electric motor the size of a softball can easily do 2 horsepower (equal to the work of two horses) of work. To gain an appreciation of how useful electric motors are, look around your home and count all the devices that contain electric motors.

PRODUCING HEAT AND LIGHT

Earlier, we learned that different materials offer different resistances to the flow of an electric current. Some materials are excellent conductors of electricity, while others are poor conductors and some do not conduct electricity at all.

The resistance of wire to electric currents causes electricity to give up some of its energy in the form of heat. This is the same principle behind the heater coil inside electric hair blow-dryers, electric water heaters, electric toasters, etc.

This same principle led to the development of the electric light bulb. The electric light bulb has had a long history going back more than three hundred years. At first, scientists were intrigued with the light given off by electric sparks. Glass tubes and balls that had their air pumped out, producing a vacuum, glowed during static electricity experiments. When batteries were invented and a steady power supply was available, large electric arcs (sparks) could be made that would give off a brilliant light as long as the current held out. You can make small similar sparks by connecting a bare wire to a lantern battery terminal and quickly tapping the other end of the wire to the other terminal.

In 1879, Thomas Edison invented the first practical electric light. He had spent two years working on an enclosed light that would light up without the fire danger of an electric arc. By trying thousands of different materials to serve as a *filament*—a thin threadlike fiber or wire inside the bulb—for his light, he finally succeeded in getting a thread coated with carbon to burn brightly for forty-five hours before it finally failed. The thread, being a poor conductor of electricity, gave off heat and light as the electricity passed through it. Modern light bulbs use the element tungsten as a filament material because it not only glows brightly but can last for many hundreds or thousands of hours. These bulbs are often called incandescent bulbs, or lights.

In the early 1900s, a new kind of lighting was invented. A gas such as neon or argon was enclosed in a glass tube. The pressure inside the tube was kept low to keep electrical resistance low. When an electric current was passed through the tube, light was produced by the interaction of the electricity with the atoms of gas. These lights, called tube lights, were adapted to store advertising in 1910. We still see this form of lighting in front of many businesses although today we usually call it neon lighting.

A second major application of tube lighting is fluorescent lighting. Inside a fluorescent tube, mercury gas gives off an invisible light called ultraviolet light when a current passes through. This light

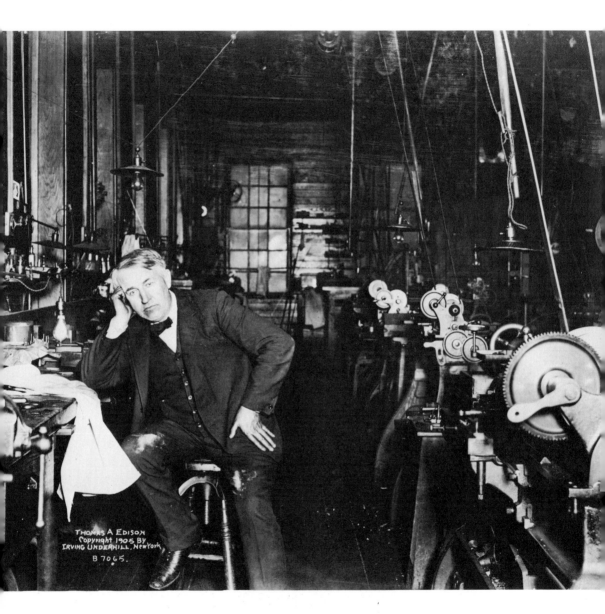

Thomas Edison

causes a white powder inside the tube wall to fluoresce, or glow brightly. Today, fluorescent lights are used in schools, businesses, and many other places because they are more efficient than incandescent light bulbs and cost less to run.

CARRYING INFORMATION

The need for communication between people at distant points may be as old as civilization itself. Many ways of communicating have been tried, including using signal fires, mirrors, drums, messenger pigeons, and cannons. While each method worked to some extent, most were restricted to "line of sight" locations where the message senders could see or hear one another, and communications were slow and often limited to brief messages. Today, all of that has changed because of electricity. When Stephen Gray learned that electricity could be transmitted, the ground was laid for the development of the telegraph and telephone.

Different telegraphs were proposed and invented by many people, but the form we are most familiar with was invented by Samuel Morse in 1837. If a wire could carry an electric current, then the current could serve as a bearer of messages.

As all inventors before and after, Morse built upon the knowledge of others. He used a simple electromagnetic receiving device that produced marks on a piece of paper when an electric current was received from the sender. The electromagnet triggered the movement of the marking device. Others had tried similar systems for telegraphs, but the equipment was complex and the transmitted messages were hard to figure out.

Morse's contribution to communications was the development of a dot and dash code that represented the letters of the alphabet and

An early electric light

his simple sending and receiving device that sent electricity along a wire to a distant city. Morse's early version of his telegraph produced short marks (dots) and long marks (dashes) on paper when a current was received from a sender. Later, the receiver was changed to a simpler electromagnetic sounder when it was learned that his telegraph operators could understand messages simply by listening to the sound of the receiver and not wait for marks to appear on paper.

Forty years after the invention of the telegraph, Alexander Graham Bell patented the first telephone. Again, electricity was used to transmit a signal along a wire. By this time much more was understood about the nature of electricity and a very sensitive current was used by Bell. The user of the telephone spoke into a microphone. Sound waves from the speaker's voice struck a thin diaphragm. Vibrations of the diaphragm produced a current that turned on and off rapidly. All the properties of the speaker's voice, such as pitch and loudness, were converted into a current by the diaphragm. This fluctuating current reached an electromagnet in the listener's earphone. The magnet turned on and off according to the fluctuations in the current. The magnetic field of the magnet caused a second diaphragm to vibrate and produce the same sound patterns as the speaker's voice.

From the invention of the telegraph and telephone, a giant leap was made in the last half of the nineteenth century with the prediction, discovery, and production of electromagnetic waves. This set the stage for the development of radio and later television, both of which rely heavily upon electricity to work.

With telegraph, telephone, radio, and television, the world rapidly changed. People could communicate almost instantly over long distances. When the space age dawned in the late 1950s, a new wrinkle was added to communication with electricity. Earth satellites were launched to serve as communication relay points in space to make all forms of communication using electricity take place more rapidly and more reliably than ever before.

Modern portable radio/cassette player

ELECTRICITY IN OUR LIVES

As we have seen, electricity is a fascinating phenomenon of nature that has immense practical applications. Before electricity went into general use by people less than 100 years ago, nearly all work was done by human or animal muscle power, steam engines, or the power of running water. Life was difficult, and the productivity of workers was low. Getting big jobs done required hundreds or thousands of people working together.

Today, we have fingertip control of the equivalent work force of hundreds or thousands of people because of electricity. We can do heavy jobs effortlessly, talk to people thousands of miles away, see moving pictures on television screens, cook food without fire, and so much more. The wonderful thing about electricity is all the ways we can put it to use. Most exciting are the applications that haven't even been thought of yet!

GLOSSARY

Alternating current (AC)—An electric current that continually alternates, or changes direction, in the wire.

Amber—A rock of hardened tree sap that produces a charge of static electricity when rubbed with fur.

Ampere—A measurement of the amount of electricity or electrons flowing past a point in one second.

Armature—A rotating coil of wire in an electric motor or generator.

Atom—The smallest particle an element can be broken down into that still retains all the properties of that element.

Battery—Two or more wet or dry cells connected together.

Bonding—A process that joins two or more atoms together by sharing some of their electrons.

Brushes—Electrical contacts that rest against, or "brush," the commutator in a motor.

Conductor—A material that makes a good pathway for electricity.

Commutator—Small metal contacts in an electric motor or generator that enable electricity to travel to or from the rotating armature.

Current electricity—Electricity in which electrons flow from one place to another.

Direct current (DC)—An electric current in which the current travels in only one direction.

Dry cell—A device for producing electricity from the reaction of pasty chemicals stored in a leakproof container.

Electricity—A form of energy originating from the charges within atoms.

Electromagnet—A device that produces a magnetic field whenever an electric current travels through it.

Electron—A small particle that orbits the nucleus of an atom.

Electroscope—A device for detecting the presence of a charge of static electricity.

Element—A substance containing only one type of atom.

Energy Efficiency Rating (EER)—A rating on appliances that states their electrical efficiency.

Field coil—A coil of wire or ring of magnets that surround the outside of an electric motor or generator.

Filament—A thin piece of wire inside a light bulb that glows when electricity passes through it.

Generator—A mechanical device for producing electricity.

Insulator—A material that resists the flow of electricity.

Ionize—A process in which an atom gains or loses an electron.

Leyden jar—A glass and metal jar that can store an electric charge.

Lodestone—*See Magnetite.*

Magnetic molecules—Molecules of certain elements that have their electrons spinning in unison so that the electron charges add up to produce a magnetic field.

Magnetism—A property of some materials and of electric currents that attracts certain metals such as iron.

Magnetite—A naturally magnetic iron ore mineral; also called lodestone.

Molecule—Two or more atoms that have bonded together.

Neutron—A particle in the nucleus of an atom that has no charge.

Nucleus—A cluster of protons and neutrons in the center of an atom.

Ohm—A measure of the resistance in an electrical circuit.

Parallel circuit—An electric circuit in which all appliances, such as light bulbs, are directly connected to the source of electricity.

Potential difference—The difference in the electrical charges between two points in an electrical circuit such as are found at the two ends of a dry cell.

Proton—A positively charged particle found in the nucleus of an atom.

Resistance—The opposition to the flow of electricity.

Series circuit—An electrical circuit in which each appliance, such as light bulbs, is connected together so that the electricity must pass through each of them in order to complete the circuit.

Solenoid—A coil of wire that produces a magnetic field when a current of electricity passes through it.

Static electricity—A form of electricity in which electrons come to rest.

Subatomic particles—The particles that make up atoms.

Turbine—A fanlike device that uses the energy in moving water or steam to turn electrical generators.

Van de Graaff generator—A static electricity machine invented by Robert Van de Graaff.

Voltage—A measure of the potential difference or "electrical pressure" in an electric circuit or electricity producing device.

Watt—A measurement unit for power.

Wet cell—A device that produces electricity from the reaction of liquid chemicals on two different metals.

Wimshurst machine—A static electricity machine invented by James Wimshurst.

BIBLIOGRAPHY

To learn more about electricity and for further ideas for electricity experiments, look up some of the following books in your school or public library.

Cherrier, Francois. *Fascinating Experiments in Physics*. New York: Sterling, 1978.

Cobb, Vickie, and Darling, Kathy. *Bet You Can't! Science Impossibilities to Fool You.* New York: Lothrop, Lee and Shepard, 1980.

Leon, George deLucenay. *The Electricity Story: 2,500 Years of Experiments and Discoveries.* New York: Arco, 1983.

Math, Irwin. *Wires and Watts, Understanding and Using Electricity.* New York: Charles Scribner's Sons, 1981.

Sootin, Harry. *Experiments With Electric Currents.* New York: Grosset and Dunlap, 1969.

_____. *Experiments With Static Electricity.* New York: W.W. Norton, 1969.

Van de Water, Marjorie. *Edison Experiments You Can Do: Based on the Original Notebooks by Thomas Alva Edison.* New York: Harper and Row, 1960.

INDEX

ABOUT THE AUTHOR

Gregory Vogt is director of the Science, Economics, and Technology Center in Milwaukee, Wisconsin. Formerly he was an aerospace education specialist at the National Aeronautics and Space Administration, a science teacher, and a planetarium lecturer. Mr. Vogt has written several other books for Franklin Watts, including *The Space Shuttle*, *A Twenty-Fifth Anniversary Album of NASA*, *Mars and the Inner Planets*, and *Model Rockets*.